The Parenting Game

A Quick Start and Troubleshooting Guide for Raising Humans

By Todd and Amanda Murfitt

Copyright © 2024 Todd Murfitt
All rights reserved.

No part of this publication may be reproduced, distributed, or transmitted in any form or by any means, including photocopying, recording, or other electronic or mechanical methods, without the prior written permission of the author, except in the case of brief quotations used in reviews and certain other non-commercial uses permitted by copyright law.

This book is intended to provide general parenting tips and advice for informational purposes only. The author is not responsible for any questionable parenting hacks you attempt at 3 a.m. while sleep-deprived. Always consult with a trusted professional for specific medical, emotional, or developmental concerns.

The Parenting Game: Quick Start and Troubleshooting Guide for Raising Humans is a work of original content. Any resemblance to actual games, cheat codes, or villains is purely coincidental (though we're looking at you, Sleep Deprivation Demon).

First Edition: 2024
Published by Murfitt Elevation

ISBN 978-1-7638370-0-3

For inquiries, visit murfittelevation.com.au

For every parent brave enough to enter The Parenting Game without a pause button or cheat codes.

And to the tiny humans who teach us that leveling up isn't about getting it right—it's about showing up.

Table of Contents

Welcome to The Parenting Game — 1
Introduction: Press Start to Begin

Level 1: The Baby Stage (0–12 Months) — 3
Big Boss: The Sleep Deprivation Demon
Save Point: Cuddles That Recharge

Level 2: The Toddler Stage (1–3 Years) — 11
Big Boss: The Snack Bandit
Save Point: Belly Laughs During Bathtime

Level 3: The Threenager Years (3–5 Years) — 21
Big Boss: The Tantrum Tornado
Save Point: The Magic of Storytime

Level 4: The School Years (6–9 Years) — 31
Big Boss: The Homework Hydra
Save Point: Family Dinners That Actually Happen

Level 5: The Tween Years (10–12 Years) — 42
Big Boss: The Peer Pressure Phantom
Save Point: Traditions and Check-ins

Level 6: The Teen Years (13–18 Years) — 51
Big Boss: The Eye Roll Master
Cheat Codes: Active Listening and Selective Memory
Save Point: Car Rides with Unexpected Honesty

Final Boss Battle — 61
Surviving Parenthood and Keeping Your Sanity Intact

Epilogue — 68
Parenting Pro Mode: Lessons Learned and Game Over

Afterward and Resources — 69
The new '3R's'
Emergency Help (RAGE! – tear out if needed!)
Parent Power-Ups
QR Code References

Notes and Scribbles — 95

Welcome to The Parenting Game

Congratulations, Player 1! You've officially embarked on the most chaotic, hilarious, and heart-expanding adventure of your life: **parenting.** Unlike most games, there's no instruction manual, no pause button, and no option to rage quit. There are, however, plenty of glitches, villains, and epic rewards along the way—if you know where to look.

Luckily, this book is here to act as your **Quick Start Guide** for raising small humans. Whether you're holding a newborn, chasing a toddler, or negotiating with a tiny dictator over bedtime snacks, you'll find practical tips, humour, and a few cheat codes to keep you sane.

Why This Book Exists

Let's be real: parenting books can be overwhelming. Some are so heavy on the philosophy they forget parents need actual solutions. Others are so focused on survival tactics they miss the bigger picture—like the fact that this whole parenting thing is also about connection, joy, and (sometimes) sheer luck.

This book is different. It's short enough to read during nap time and packed with the kind of advice that works in the real world. It's a mix of practical, heartfelt, and humorous—because raising humans should make you laugh as much as it makes you cry.

What to Expect

This isn't a book you need to read cover to cover. Think of it as a parenting toolbox:
Facing a meltdown at bedtime? Flip to *Level 3: Threenager Chaos*.
Feeling disconnected from your kid? Skim the "Save Point" sections for quick reconnection tips.
Just need a laugh? Check out the Big Boss battles—we've all faced the Sleep Deprivation Demon.

You'll also find QR codes, quick Google-worthy prompts, and tips you can implement immediately. So, keep your device handy—you know it's within reach anyway.
Remember, parenting isn't about being perfect. It's about showing up, making mistakes, and playing the game with all your heart. Let's get started.

Press Start to Begin.

Level 1

The Baby Stage (0-12 Months)

Congratulations! You've entered **Level 1: The Baby Stage.** This is the tutorial level, where your baby arrives with minimal instructions, lots of glitches, and one primary mission: **keep them alive, figure out what they want, and survive on almost no sleep.**

It's a stage full of firsts: first cuddles, first sleepless nights, and your first realization that nappy blowouts are nature's cruellest prank. But it's also the stage where you'll start building a bond with your baby that lays the foundation for every level to come. Pro tip: **Connection, not perfection, is the goal here.** Every time you show up for your baby—even when you're exhausted, clueless, or covered in spit-up—you're teaching them that they can trust you. And that's the cheat code for successful parenting.

Core Mission: Build the Bond

At this stage, your baby has one primary concern: **"Is someone here for me?"** Their survival instincts depend on you responding to their cries, holding them close, and figuring out what they need. When you do, you're not just meeting their basic needs—you're building trust, creating emotional security, and literally wiring their little brain for connection.

But here's the secret: Connection doesn't require expensive gadgets or expert-level parenting skills. It's in the small, everyday moments:

- When you lock eyes during a midnight feeding.
- When you hum a tune while rocking them to sleep.
- When you comfort their cries, even when you're running on fumes.

These moments might feel mundane, but they're powerful. Every cuddle, every goofy face, and every whispered "we've got this", strengthens your bond and teaches your baby the world is safe.

Big Boss Battle: The Sleep Deprivation Demon

This villain lurks in every corner, ready to strike the moment you think you've got things under control. It thrives on chaos, clouding your judgment, sapping your energy, and convincing you that you're failing.

- **Defeat Strategy:**
    1. **Tag Team Mode:** Divide and conquer. If you have a co-player (partner, parent, or friend), take turns on night shifts so you both get some sleep.
    2. **Power Nap Buff:** Nap when the baby naps. Yes, it's a cliché, but it works—15 minutes can feel like a game changer.
    3. **Summon Allies:** Call in reinforcements. A grandparent, a neighbour, or even a delivery driver bearing coffee can be your MVP.

 Pro tip: Perfectionism has no place in this battle. Your only goal is survival—and that's a win.

Gameplay Hazards

- **The Crying Glitch:**
Babies cry—it's their way of communicating. Sometimes it's obvious (hunger, wet nappy), and sometimes it's a mystery.
    - **Fix:** Run the troubleshooting checklist:
        1. Is the baby hungry?
        2. Are they wet or dirty?
        3. Are they tired or overstimulated?
        4. **Try the 5 S's**: Swaddle, Side position, Shush, Swing, Suck (a pacifier or feed).

- **The Advice Avalanche:**
Everyone from strangers in the grocery store to your great-aunt will have opinions about how you should raise your baby.
    - **Fix:** Think of their advice as side quests—you don't have to accept every one. Smile, nod, and stick to wh   ou.

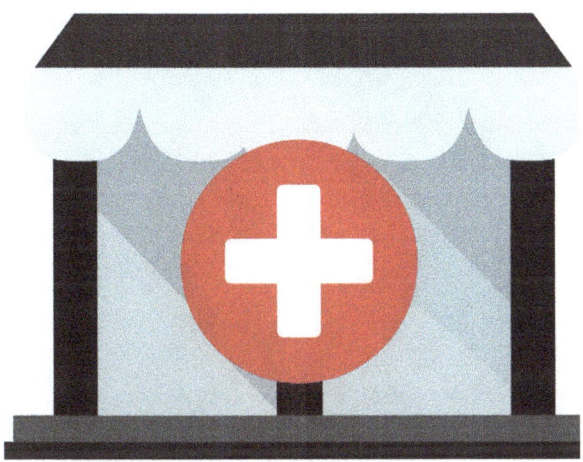

Cheat Codes for Level 1

1. **The White Noise Buff:**
   White noise machines (or apps) are magical tools that mimic the womb's comforting sounds and help babies (and you) sleep better. Bonus points if it also drowns out background noise like barking dogs or Netflix marathons.

2. **One-Handed Ninja Skill:**
   Master the art of doing everything one-handed while holding a baby. Eating, brushing your teeth, and even folding laundry are possible with practice—and maybe a baby carrier.

3. **Cuddle Reset Button:**
   Feeling overwhelmed? Hold your baby close and breathe together. Physical contact is calming for both of you and often resets the moment.

Save Point: The Power of Pause

Amid the chaos, there will be moments that take your breath away. Your baby's tiny fingers wrapped around yours, holding on like you're their whole world. The way they relax completely against your chest when they fall asleep, their soft breaths syncing with yours, creating a rhythm of calm in the middle of the storm.

These moments are your **Save Point**—a chance to pause, recharge, and remember why this stage, exhausting as it is, is also magical. They remind you that, despite the messiness and sleepless nights, you are building something extraordinary. In those quiet, fleeting seconds, time seems to stand still. You're not just surviving—you're connecting and shaping a little human who trusts you completely. Let these moments fuel you through the tough days and remind you why it's all worth it.

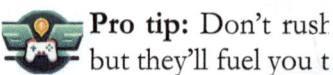 **Pro tip:** Don't rush ̇ ̇oments. They're fleeting, but they'll fuel you t ̇ boss battle ahead.

Side Quests!

TUMMY TIME TREASURE HUNT:

- **Objective:** Help your baby build strength during tummy time.
- **How to Play:** Lay your baby on a soft surface and place colourful toys or a mirror within reach. Cheer them on as they lift their head or wiggle toward the objects.
- **Reward:** A stronger baby and joyful moments as you encourage their progress.

LULLABY REMIX QUEST:

- **Objective:** Create a personalized lullaby for your baby.
- **How to Play:** Use their name or funny rhymes in a simple tune. Sing it during bedtime or fussy moments.
- **Reward:** A calming bedtime ritual that becomes a special bonding moment.

Troubleshooting Guide

Issue	Fix
My baby only sleeps during the day, not at night.	Help them distinguish day from night by keeping daytime bright and active, and nighttime dark and quiet.
They're crying, but I've checked everything.	Sometimes babies cry to release tension. Hold them close and offer comfort—it's okay if they don't stop immediately.
I'm overwhelmed by advice from everyone.	Politely thank people for their input, then trust your instincts. Not every piece of advice is meant for you or your baby.
They won't latch during breastfeeding.	Consult a lactation consultant or try different positions. Remember, fed is best—whether it's breast milk, formula, or a combination.
They scream during nappy changes.	Distract them with a small toy or sing a silly song. A warm wipe can also help if they're startled by the cold.
I feel like I'm failing as a parent.	You're not. Parenting is hard, and perfection isn't the goal. Celebrate small wins and remind yourself that showing up is what matters most.
I never get time for myself.	Build short self-care moments into your day—a 10-minute shower, a cup of tea, or guilt-free scrolling while the baby naps.
My baby hates tummy time.	Start small, even 30 seconds, and make it fun with toys or your face at their level. Try tummy time on your chest if the floor is too overwhelming.

Pro Tip for Cheat Codes and Troubleshooting

Remember: every baby is different. What works one day might not work the next, and that's okay. Keep experimenting, stay flexible, and trust that you're learning the game as you go.

Level 2

The Toddler Stage (1-3 Years)

Congratulations! You've levelled up to **The Toddler Stage**, where your baby transforms into a highly mobile, snack-demanding mini-boss with a flair for drama. This stage is like entering the open-world portion of the game: your toddler has free roam and zero impulse control. Your primary missions? **Survive tantrums, manage chaos, and encourage independence (without losing your mind).**

 Pro tip: Toddlers don't come with a pause button, but they do come with an infinite capacity for wonder. Lean into the chaos, laugh often, and always keep snacks on hand.

Core Mission: Independence

Toddlers are explorers by nature, which is a polite way of saying they will try to dismantle your home. They're also determined to prove they don't need you—except when they absolutely do (which is every 4.2 minutes). Your job is to help them feel safe while they figure out how to be their own little person.

How to foster independence:

1. **Offer choices:**
    - Toddlers love control, so give it to them in small, manageable doses: "Do you want the red cup or the blue cup?"
2. **Encourage self-help:**
    - Celebrate every attempt to dress themselves, even if their pants are on backward and their shirt is inside out.

3. **Let them lead (within reason):**
    - A 10-minute walk might take 30 minutes because they're busy examining every rock and leaf. That's okay—they're learning about the world.

 Pro tip: Toddlers thrive on routine, so create a daily structure that balances exploration with predictability. Think of it as their "game map."

Big Boss Battle: The Snack Bandit

This villain lurks in your kitchen, demanding crackers, cookies, or the one snack you don't have in stock. The Snack Bandit strikes at the worst times: right before meals, in the middle of grocery store trips, and during car rides when you're out of reach of your stash.

- **Defeat Strategy:**
    1. **Preload Inventory:** Keep a "snack arsenal" in every bag, pocket, and glove compartment. Think easy-to-grab, low-mess options like fruit pouches or pretzels.
    2. **Limit Power-Ups:** Snacks are fine, but don't let them replace meals. Set snack windows and stick to them.
    3. **Diversion Tactics:** When the Snack Bandit strikes outside of snack time, redirect: "How about a dance party instead?"

Pro tip: Toddlers don't snack because they're hungry. They snack because they're bored. Be one step ahead.

Gameplay Hazards

- **The "No!" Monster:**
  Your toddler has discovered their favourite word, and it's "No." They'll use it for everything—from getting dressed to eating dinner.
    - **Fix:** Turn "No" into a game: "I bet you can't say 'Yes?'" Or offer two choices, so "No" isn't an option.

- **The Sudden Meltdown Bug:**
  Meltdowns happen, often with no warning and over things like "wrong colour socks."
    - **Fix:** Stay calm and validate their feelings: "I see you're upset because the blue socks are in the wash. That's hard." Then distract or redirect as needed.

- **The Childcare Conundrum:**

    Deciding on childcare feels overwhelming, and guilt creeps in whether you choose daycare, a nanny, or a family member.

    - **Fix:** Childcare isn't about replacing you; it's about finding the right support system for your family. Visit options, trust your gut, and remember that your love and connection at home remain the foundation of your child's security.
    - **Reassurance:** Choosing childcare doesn't make you a bad parent—it makes you a resourceful one. What matters most is that your child feels safe and supported.

watch

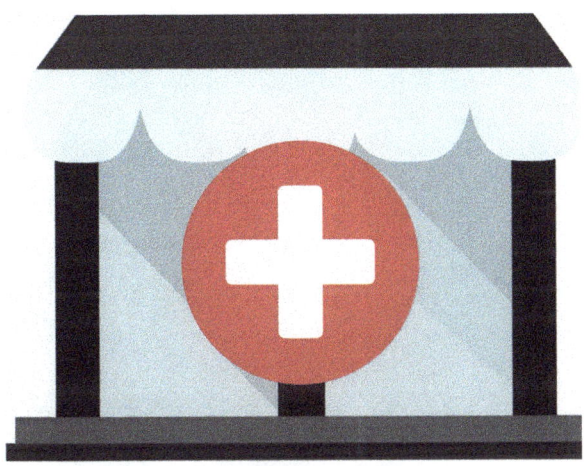

Cheat Codes for Level 2

1. **Sticker Chart Magic:**
   Motivation is everything. Create a sticker chart for tasks like brushing teeth or tidying toys. Toddlers will do almost anything for a shiny sticker.

2. **Pre-emptive Distraction:**
   Keep a rotation of small toys or books on hand for tantrum-prevention. Pro tip: Only pull them out during emergencies to keep them novel.

3. **Screen Time: The Double-Edged Sword:**
   Screen time can save your sanity but use it wisely. Choose educational shows (hello, *Bluey*!) and set clear limits to avoid the Screen Time Monster.

Save Point: The Belly Laugh Reset

Few things are as healing as a toddler's belly laugh. The pure joy that bursts forth when you blow raspberries on their tummy or make silly faces during bath time can brighten even the hardest days. Their laughter is infectious, melting away stress and fatigue in an instant.

These moments are your **Save Point**—a chance to pause amidst the whirlwind of toddlerhood and soak in the delight of this stage. They remind you that despite the tantrums and messes, this time is filled with magic. Let these joyful sounds recharge your spirit and remind you why this stage, as chaotic as it is, is also pure joy.

 Pro tip: Don't underestimate the power of your own laughter. Laughing with your toddler is a shortcut to connection—and sanity.

Side Quests!

Treasure Hunt Adventure:

- **Objective:** Create a scavenger hunt for your toddler using toys or snacks as "treasures."
- **How to Play:** Hide items around the house and give simple clues to help your toddler find them.
- **Reward:** Boosts problem-solving skills and creates excitement.

Dance-Off Showdown:

- **Objective:** Have a 5-minute dance party with your toddler.
- **How to Play:** Play their favourite songs and get silly with your moves. Let them lead the choreography.
- **Reward:** Burn off energy and create joyful memories together.

 # Troubleshooting Guide

Issue	Fix
My toddler throws food during meals.	Keep meal portions small and introduce a "no thank you" bowl for unwanted food to redirect the behaviour.
They say "no" to everything.	Offer two choices instead of yes/no questions: "Do you want the red shirt or the blue one?" Giving them control reduces power struggles.
They have meltdowns over small things.	Stay calm and acknowledge their feelings: "I see you're upset because the tower fell. That's hard." Then offer a distraction or solution.
They refuse to share with others.	Focus on turn-taking rather than sharing. "You can play with the truck for two minutes, then it's your friend's turn."
Bedtime is a battle every night.	Establish a consistent bedtime routine: bath, story, and lights out. Keep it calm and predictable to reduce resistance.
They won't sit still for anything.	Channel their energy into short, active tasks like fetching a toy or jumping on a pillow before transitioning to quieter activities.
They want to do everything themselves.	Let them try! Offer safe opportunities for independence, even if it's messy. "You can pour your cereal, and I'll help with the milk."
They bite or hit when frustrated.	Stay calm, remove them from the situation, and explain: "We don't bite. Let's use words to tell me how you're feeling."

 Pro Tip for Cheat Codes and Troubleshooting

Toddlers thrive on structure and positive reinforcement. When things feel chaotic, focus on connection and consistency—they're learning, not defying.

Level 3

The Threenager Years (3-5 Years)

Congratulations, Player 1, you've unlocked **The Threenager Years**, where your toddler's sass reaches new heights, their emotions have no speed limit, and their negotiating skills rival those of seasoned lawyers. This level is all about navigating big personalities, bigger emotions, and the occasional full-volume meltdown in public.

Your primary mission: **Survive the chaos while fostering their creativity, independence, and growing sense of self.**

 **Pro tip:** Threenagers are like mini volcanos—unpredictable and explosive, but also capable of creating beautiful moments of awe. The key is to weather the eruptions and treasure the quiet moments in between.

Core Mission: Embrace the Drama and Build Emo   'esilience

At this stage, your child is developing emotional depth and independence but lacks the tools to manage those big feelings. This is where you step in—not to fix everything, but to guide them in understanding and expressing their emotions.

How to build resilience:

1. **Label Their Feelings:**
    - "I see you're frustrated because the block tower fell. That's hard."
    - Naming emotions helps them feel seen, normalises feelings and teaches them to express themselves.

2. **Model Emotional Regulation:**
    - If you stay calm during their meltdowns, you're showing them how to handle stress. (Easier said than done, I know!)
3. **Play it Out:**
    - Creative play is their language. Whether it's a puppet show about sharing or using toys to talk through fears, play can help them process emotions.

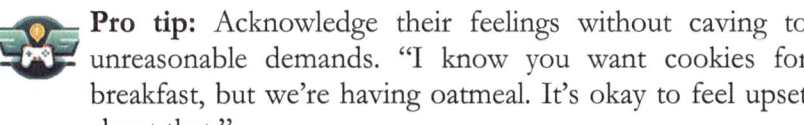 **Pro tip:** Acknowledge their feelings without caving to unreasonable demands. "I know you want cookies for breakfast, but we're having oatmeal. It's okay to feel upset about that."

  Listen

Big Boss Battle: The Tantrum Tornado

The Tantrum Tornado hits without warning, often because the toast was cut into triangles instead of squares. These emotional storms can feel endless, but they're not personal—they're part of your child's learning curve.

- **Defeat Strategy:**
    1. **Stay Calm:** Your calm presence helps them regulate. Take deep breaths, even if they're screaming at full volume.
    2. **Set Boundaries:** Let them feel their feelings but hold firm on limits. "I won't let you throw toys, but I'll stay with you until you're ready to calm down."
    3. **Redirect Energy:** When the tornado starts to fizzle, offer a distraction: "Want to help me feed the dog?"

Pro tip: Remember, tantrums are a sign of a healthy, growing brain learning to handle frustration. Your job is to guide, not control.

Gameplay Hazards

- **The Question Loop:**
  "Why? Why? Why?" Your child has entered the infinite loop of curiosity, and it's adorable... until it's not.
    - **Fix:** Answer simply, then redirect: "Why does the sun shine? Great question! Let's draw the sun while we talk about it."

- **The Sharing Struggle:**
  Sharing doesn't come naturally to threenagers. "MINE!" is their battle cry.
    - **Fix:** Focus on turn-taking instead of sharing: "You can play with the truck for two minutes, then it's your friend's turn."

- **The Bedtime Procrastinator:**
  Just as you're ready to collapse, your threenager suddenly needs water, a story, and an existential discussion about dinosaurs.
    - **Fix:** Set a consistent bedtime routine and stick to it: "One drink, one story, then lights out."

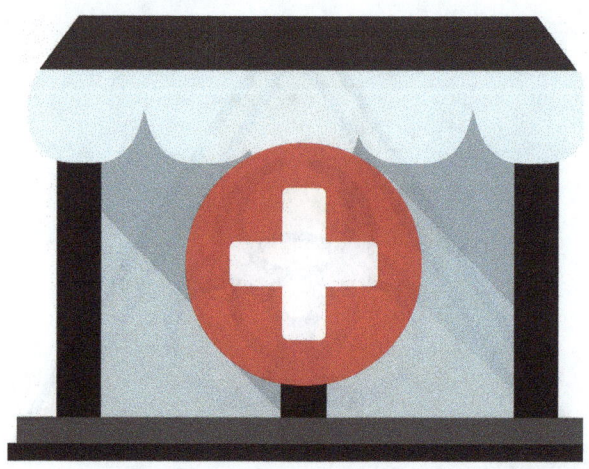

Cheat Codes for Level 3

1. **The Silly Distraction Buff:**
   Threenagers can't resist laughter. Use silly voices or exaggerated movements to diffuse tension during tricky moments.

2. **The Snack Negotiation Tactic:**
   Snacks solve 80% of minor crises. Keep a stash of crackers, fruit, or raisins to prevent meltdowns before they start.

3. **The Praise Power-Up:**
   Catch them being good and celebrate it: "I love how you helped clean up your toys!" Positive reinforcement builds cooperation.

Save Point: The Magic of Storytime

Storytime isn't just about books—it's about connection. Whether you're snuggled on the couch, their head resting on your shoulder, or acting out silly characters that make them giggle uncontrollably, these moments go beyond words on a page. They're about creating a safe, comforting ritual that strengthens your bond.

As you read together, you're not only building their vocabulary and imagination but also showing them that your time and attention are theirs. Storytime becomes a sanctuary from the busyness of life, a pause button that lets you both recharge and be fully present with each other.

These moments may seem small, but they lay the foundation for a love of learning, laughter, and connection. So, grab a book, make it silly, and savour the magic of being together.

 Pro tip: Choose books that reflect their experiences and feelings. Stories about bravery, friendship, and emotions can help them process their world.

Side Quests!

BLOCK TOWER CHALLENGE:

- **Objective:** Build the tallest block tower together.
- **How to Play:** Take turns adding blocks, encouraging teamwork. Cheer them on even when the tower topples.
- **Reward:** Encourages patience, teamwork, and a sense of achievement.

STORY CREATOR MISSION:

- **Objective:** Make up a story together.
- **How to Play:** Take turns adding a sentence or act it out with toys. Draw pictures to go with the story if your child enjoys art.
- **Reward:** Boosts creativity and strengthens language skills.

Troubleshooting Guide

Issue	Fix
My child says "no" to everything, even things they want.	Stay calm and reframe requests as statements or fun challenges: "Time to race to the car!" or "Let's see if you can pick up your toys faster than me!"
They have constant tantrums over small things.	Acknowledge their feelings: "I see you're upset because your block tower fell." Redirect their focus or offer a simple solution to help them reset.
They won't share with siblings or friends.	Practice turn-taking instead of forcing sharing. "You can play with the car for two minutes, then it's your friend's turn."
They constantly interrupt conversations.	Teach them to wait their turn by introducing a simple signal (like holding your hand) to show they want to speak. Praise them when they succeed.
Bedtime takes forever because of stalling.	Keep bedtime routines consistent and set clear boundaries: "One story, then lights out." Use a timer to signal transitions.
They argue over every little thing.	Avoid power struggles by offering limited choices: "Do you want to wear the red shoes or the blue ones?" This gives them a sense of control.
They seem clingy or afraid to try new things.	Encourage small steps toward independence. Stay nearby to offer reassurance but celebrate their efforts when they take the initiative.
They whine instead of asking politely.	Model the behaviour you want to see. Gently prompt them: "Can you ask in a calm voice? Say, 'Can I have a snack, please?'"

Pro Tip for Troubleshooting

Threenagers are learning to navigate their big feelings and growing independence. Your calm, consistent guidance teaches them that they're safe to explore and express themselves—even when emotions run high.

Level 4

The School Years (6-9 Years)

Congratulations, Player 1, you've reached **The School Years**, where your child embarks on quests for knowledge, friendships, and independence. This level introduces new challenges like navigating social dynamics, homework battles, and the occasional showdown with The Comparison Monster. Your mission? **Guide your player toward confidence, resilience, and a lifelong love of learning—without losing your sanity.**

Pro tip: **The School Years are a balance of structure and play.** Encourage exploration while providing guardrails. They'll thank you someday—probably not today, though.

Core Mission: Build Confidence and Resilience

At this stage, your child starts facing "real-world" challenges, from understanding fractions to figuring out playground politics. Your job is to be their co-pilot, offering guidance while letting them take the controls.

How to build confidence and resilience:

1. **Celebrate Effort Over Results:**
    - Praise their hard work, not just their wins. "You worked so hard on that project—I'm proud of you! How do you feel about that?"
2. **Let Them Solve Problems:**
    - Resist the urge to swoop in. Instead, ask questions: "What do you think you could do next?"

3. **Teach Them to Fail Forward:**
    - Normalise mistakes as part of learning. Share your own failures and what you learned from them.

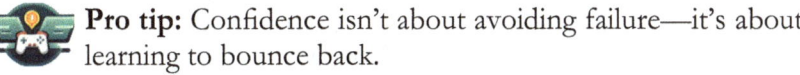 **Pro tip:** Confidence isn't about avoiding failure—it's about learning to bounce back.

Big Boss: The Homework Hydra

The Homework Hydra is a multi-headed beast that sprouts a new challenge each night. Just when you think you've conquered maths, it rears its head with spelling lists and science projects.

- **Defeat Strategy:**
    1. **Create a Homework Zone:** A distraction-free area with all the supplies they need.
    2. **Break It Down:** Help them tackle one head of the Hydra at a time. "Let's do 10 minutes of reading, then take a break."
    3. **Offer Support, Not Solutions:** Guide them, but let them do the work. "I'm here if you need help, but I know you've got this!"

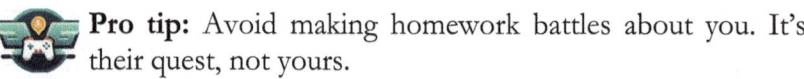 **Pro tip:** Avoid making homework battles about you. It's their quest, not yours.

Gameplay Hazards

- **The Comparison Monster:**
  The Comparison Monster lurks at learner conversations and birthday parties, whispering that your child should be smarter, faster, or better at piano than their peers.
    - **Fix:** Focus on your child's unique strengths and celebrate their progress. Remind yourself (and them) that everyone levels up at their own pace.

- **The "I Forgot" Glitch:**
  Your child will forget homework assignments, lunches, and occasionally their shoes.
    - **Fix:** Teach them to use calendars, checklists, or reminder apps to build responsibility.

- **The FOMO Goblin:**
  Fear of Missing Out hits hard in the School Years, especially when every friend seems to have the latest gadget or attend the coolest camp.
    - **Fix:** Set boundaries around wants versus needs. "I know you really want that game console, but let's save up for it together."

- **The School Choice Showdown**

  Debates about private, public, or alternative schooling leave you doubting your decisions and worrying about your child's future.
    - **Fix:** The "best" school is the one that fits your child's needs and your family's values. Tour schools, meet teachers, and focus on environments where your child will feel supported.
    - **Reassurance:** No school is perfect, and your involvement as a parent has a bigger impact than any institution. You're not locked into one path—stay adaptable.

watch

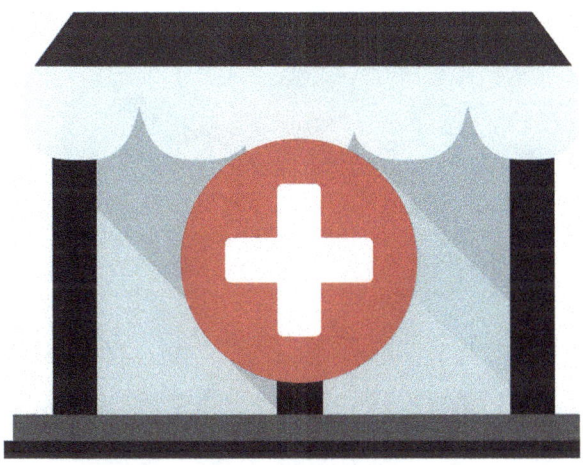

Cheat Codes for Level 4

1. **Family Meeting Power-Up:**
   Weekly check-ins help everyone stay on the same page about schedules, goals, and responsibilities. Bonus: It models teamwork.

2. **Gamify Chores:**
   Turn chores into quests with rewards for completion. "Clean your room to earn 50 XP toward an ice cream outing!"

3. **Bedtime Wind-Down Ritual:**
   Create a calming routine—reading, talking about their day, or sharing three things they're grateful for. It helps them process the day and builds connection.

Save Point: Family Dinners That Actually Happen

Life gets busy, but family meals—even just once or twice a week—are like a reset button. They offer a chance to slow down, connect, and be fully present with each other. Whether it's a quick breakfast before school or a dinner where everyone shares their day, these moments are about more than just food.

Use this time to share stories, laugh together, and let your child know they're part of something bigger—a family that values time spent together. It doesn't have to be perfect; even takeout at the kitchen table counts. What matters most is the connection you create and the memories you build, one meal at a time.

In the chaos of life, family meals are a small but powerful way to recharge as a team.

 Pro tip: Keep it simple. It's not about the food—it's about the connection.

Side Quests!

Homework Helper Guild:

- **Objective:** Support your child during homework time.
- **How to Play:** Sit with them, ask questions, and encourage their efforts.
- **Reward:** Builds their confidence and reinforces that learning is a team effort.

DIY Game Night:

- **Objective:** Create a simple board game together.
- **How to Play:** Use paper, pencils and dice to invent a game with your own rules. Play as a family and tweak as you go.
- **Reward:** Encourages creativity and brings the family together.

 # Troubleshooting Guide

Issue	Fix
My child refuses to do homework.	Break tasks into smaller chunks and offer short breaks between. Use positive reinforcement: "Once this is done, we can play your favourite game!"
They compare themselves to others.	Highlight their unique strengths and focus on effort over results: "You worked so hard on that project—I'm so proud of you!"
They resist helping with chores.	Turn chores into games or use incentives like sticker charts: "Let's see how fast we can pick up the toys!"
They struggle to make friends at school.	Role-play common social situations and teach them conversation starters: "Hi, can I play with you?"
They won't put down screens to join family activities.	Set clear screen-time limits and create screen-free zones, like during meals or family time. Offer engaging alternatives like a family board game.
They complain about being bored all the time.	Encourage creativity by suggesting open-ended activities like building with blocks or drawing. Let them know it's okay to feel bored sometimes—it sparks creativity.
They struggle with losing games or competitions.	Model good sportsmanship and emphasize the fun of playing, not just winning. Praise their effort and teamwork.
They are afraid to try new activities.	Start small and offer encouragement: "I know it feels scary, but let's try it together." Celebrate their bravery, even if they only take the first step.

Pro Tip for Troubleshooting

The school years are about building confidence and resilience. Celebrate their small wins, guide them through challenges, and remind them that their worth isn't tied to their performance but to who they are.

Level 5

The Tween Years (10-12 Years)

Congratulations, Player 1, you've reached **The Tween Years**, a level that feels like a bridge between childhood and the teenage gauntlet. This stage comes with a mix of budding independence, heightened curiosity, and, yes, a bit of sass. Your mission? To help your tween navigate this transitional time with confidence while keeping the lines of connection strong.

At this level, your tween is figuring out who they are, testing boundaries, and beginning to care deeply about what their peers think. It's a time of self-discovery, but it's also a time when they need your guidance, even if they pretend they don't. Think of this level as a co-op mission: you're there to help them navigate the game, even if they sometimes want to play solo.

 Pro tip: Tweens often open up in unexpected moments—while folding laundry, or while gaming together. Create space for natural conversations without forcing them.

Core Mission: Fostering Independence While Staying Connected

Tweens are starting to seek independence, but they still need you as their anchor. Your job is to give them room to explore while keeping them tethered to the values and support systems that will guide them through tougher levels ahead. Connection doesn't mean micromanaging—it means being their safe base when they need advice, reassurance, or a reminder of who they are.

 Pro tip: Focus on celebrating their hard work rather than the end result. This helps them build confidence in their abilities, even when things don't go perfectly.

Big Boss Battle: The Peer Pressure Phantom

The **Peer Pressure Phantom** thrives in the shadows of insecurity and the desire to fit in. It whispers doubts and tempts your tween to prioritize acceptance over authenticity. Whether it's about joining social media, wearing the "right" clothes, or trying something they're not ready for, this boss feeds on their fear of standing out.

- **Defeat Strategy:**
    1. **Equip Them with Tools:** Teach them how to say no and practice self-advocacy. Role-playing different scenarios can give them confidence.
    2. **Talk About It Before It Happens:** Have open discussions about peer pressure and share stories from your own life.
    3. **Reinforce Their Strengths:** Celebrate their unique qualities and help them feel good about who they are.

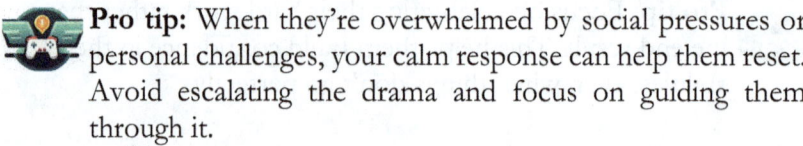

Pro tip: When they're overwhelmed by social pressures or personal challenges, your calm response can help them reset. Avoid escalating the drama and focus on guiding them through it.

Gameplay Hazards

1. **The Drama Cyclone:**
   Friendship conflicts can blow up over minor issues, leaving your tween feeling overwhelmed.
   Fix: Teach them to pause and process emotions before reacting. Help them see multiple perspectives to build empathy and conflict-resolution skills.

2. **The Motivation Gremlin:**
   Tweens may avoid responsibilities like chores or homework in favour of easier, more enjoyable distractions.
   - **Fix:** Break tasks into smaller steps, make them fun (like challenges or competitions), and reinforce effort with positive feedback.

3. **The Confidence Crusher:**
   Tweens might compare themselves to others, leading to self-doubt or lowered self-esteem.
   - **Fix:** Focus on their strengths and unique qualities. Teach them that social media often portrays an unrealistic version of life.

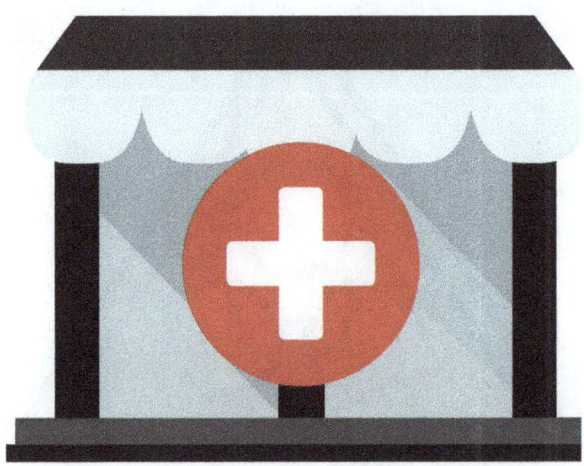

Cheat Codes for Level 5

1. **Ask for Their Opinions:**
   - Get their input on family decisions, like planning outings or choosing a new hobby. It makes them feel valued and encourages critical thinking.

2. **Normalize Mistakes:**
   - Share your own missteps and how you recovered. This teaches them that failure is a normal part of learning and growth.

3. **Tech-Free Time Together:**
   - Create regular "no devices" zones during meals, family activities, or bedtime to foster meaningful face-to-face connection.

Save Point: Traditions and Check-ins

Even as your tween pulls away to explore their world, they need the stability of predictable moments with you. Save Points in this level might look like:

- Weekly traditions, like Sunday pancakes or Friday movie nights.
- A short daily check-in, where you ask, "What was the best part of your day?"

These rituals act as anchors, grounding your tween in the knowledge that no matter how big their world gets, your connection is always there.

Pro tip: Help your tween develop self-regulation by encouraging them to pause before reacting—whether it's to a friendship drama or a frustrating challenge. This builds emotional resilience.

Side Quests!

Family Debate Night

- **Objective:** Encourage critical thinking by debating fun, low-stakes topics like "Which superpower is better: flying or invisibility?"
- **Reward:** Builds confidence in expressing opinions and develops reasoning skills.

Shared Creative Project

- **Objective:** Collaborate on a long-term project like a photo album, scrapbook, or DIY craft.
- **Reward:** Strengthens teamwork and fosters a sense of accomplishment.

Troubleshooting Guide

Issue	Fix
They don't talk to me as much.	Create low-pressure moments for connection, like car rides or cooking together. Avoid grilling them with questions—let them come to you naturally.
They seem obsessed with fitting in.	Reinforce their individuality by celebrating their unique traits. Share stories of times when staying true to yourself worked in your favour.
They're glued to their devices.	Set clear boundaries for screen time and enforce "tech-free" family moments. Model healthy tech habits yourself to lead by example.
They roll their eyes at everything I say.	Don't take it personally—it's often a tween's way of asserting independence. Respond with humour or empathy to keep the connection alive.
They're always comparing themselves to others.	Help them focus on their personal strengths and successes. Discuss how social media often portrays a filtered, unrealistic version of life.
Friendship drama takes over their life.	Teach them to pause before reacting and encourage open communication with friends. Help them see conflicts from multiple perspectives.
They avoid responsibility.	Break tasks into smaller steps and offer positive reinforcement for completing them. Make it fun by turning chores into challenges or competitions.
They struggle with self-esteem.	Remind them of their accomplishments and encourage them to try new things.

| | Avoid over-praising and focus on effort over results. |

 Pro Tip for Troubleshooting

Tweens are testing their independence, but they still need your presence, patience, and guidance. The trick is to stay available without smothering them. Show interest in their hobbies, listen when they want to talk, and offer support when they stumble. Your steady presence will help them build the confidence they need to tackle the next level.

Level 6

The Teen Years (13-18 Years)

Congratulations, Player 1, you've reached **The Teen Years**, where your child transforms into a highly skilled, fiercely independent, and occasionally eye-rolling master of sarcasm. This level is a tricky balance between letting them explore their independence and staying connected as they navigate the complexities of growing up in a digital world.

Your primary mission: **Maintain real connection in the face of increasing distractions, guide them through social and emotional challenges, and equip them to level up to adulthood.**

Pro tip: Teenagers don't need you to fix everything—they need you to listen, respect their growing autonomy, and remind them you're always in their corner.

Core Mission: Prioritise Real Connection Over Virtual Noise

Teenagers live in a hyper-connected world, but ironically, that often leads to disconnection. Social media, devices, and online games compete for their attention, but nothing replaces real, face-to-face connection. Your challenge is to stay relevant and engaged in their lives without invading their growing independence.

How to build real connection:
1. **Be Present Without Hovering:**
    o Show up for the important stuff—sports games, performances, late-night chats—but give them space to be themselves.
2. **Model Healthy Screen Habits:**
    o Teens will mimic what they see. If you're glued to your phone, they will be too. Create device-free zones like family dinners or car rides.

3. **Ask Open-Ended Questions:**
    o Move beyond "How was school?" and try, "What's something interesting that happened today?" or "What's your favourite thing about that game you're playing?"

Pro tip: The moments they decide to open up might not be convenient, but they're golden. Be ready to drop what you're doing when they start talking.

Listen

Big Boss Battle: The Eye Roll Master

The Eye Roll Master strikes whenever you try to offer advice, make a joke, or even exist in their general vicinity. Its powers include sarcasm, dramatic sighs, and a remarkable ability to make you question your parenting skills.

- **Defeat Strategy:**
    1. **Don't Take It Personally:** Remember, their frustration is often about their own struggles, not you.
    2. **Stay Curious:** Respond to snark with genuine curiosity. "That's an interesting take—tell me more."
    3. **Pick Your Battles:** Focus on the big issues (safety, respect) and let smaller annoyances slide.

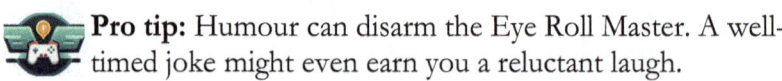 **Pro tip:** Humour can disarm the Eye Roll Master. A well-timed joke might even earn you a reluctant laugh.

Gameplay Hazards

- **The Social Media Siren:**
  This seductive villain lures teens into hours of scrolling, comparing, and chasing likes, often leaving them feeling inadequate.
    - **Fix:** Talk openly about the curated nature of social media and encourage breaks. "It's okay to unplug—it doesn't mean you're missing out."

- **The Peer Pressure Phantom:**
  This shadowy figure thrives on FOMO and the fear of not fitting in.
    - **Fix:** Teach them to trust their instincts. Role-play tricky scenarios so they feel prepared to say no while saving face.

- **The Device Addiction Gremlin:**
  Screen time creeps into every corner of life, from late-night texting to endless gaming marathons.
    - **Fix:** Set clear limits on device usage and encourage non-digital hobbies like sports, art, or volunteering.

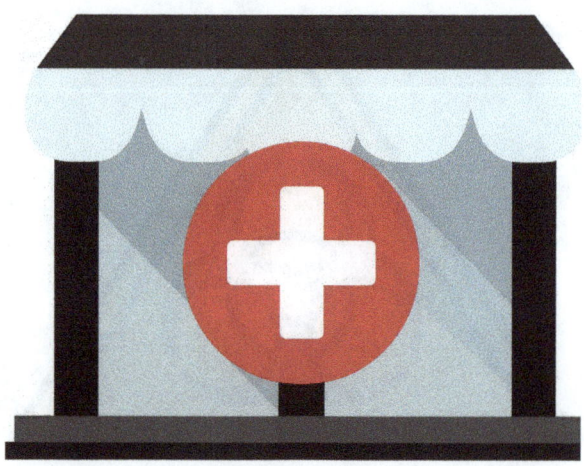

Cheat Codes for Level 6

1. **The Car Ride Confessional:**
   Teens often open up during car rides because there's no eye contact. Use these moments to have deeper conversations.

2. **The "Yes" Buffer:**
   When they ask for freedom or privileges, default to "Let me think about it" instead of an automatic no. It shows you respect their autonomy while giving you time to decide.

3. **The Fail-Safe Reaction:**
   When they mess up (and they will), focus on problem-solving rather than punishment: "What can we do to fix this?"

Save Point: Car Rides with Unexpected Honesty

The car is a magical place. With no distractions and no direct eye contact, teens often feel more comfortable letting their guard down. It's a space where conversations can flow naturally, free from the pressure of face-to-face interactions.

Use this time to truly listen—without judgment, interruption, or the urge to solve every problem. Sometimes, they just need to be heard. Ask open-ended questions or simply wait for them to speak when they're ready. Even silence can be meaningful; it shows you're there, present, and available.

These small, unplanned moments can lead to some of the most meaningful connections. So next time you're on the road together, resist the temptation to fill the silence and let the magic of the car work in your favour.

 Pro tip: Don't force the conversation. Sometimes just being there is enough.

Side Quests!

PLAYLIST EXCHANGE QUEST:

- **Objective:** Create playlists for each other and share why you chose certain songs.
- **How to Play:** Spend time listening together and discussing the music.
- **Reward:** Opens up meaningful conversations and shows mutual appreciation.

PROJECT PARTNER CHALLENGE:

- **Objective:** Collaborate on something your teen is passionate about (e.g., redecorating their room, filming a video, planning a family event).
- How to Play: Let your teen take the lead while you support them.
- **Reward:** Builds trust, teamwork, and shared memories.

# Troubleshooting Guide

Issue	Fix
My teen spends all their time on their phone.	Set clear screen-time boundaries and model healthy habits yourself. Create screen-free times, like during meals or before bed.
They shut down and won't talk to me.	Give them space but let them know you're available. Use low-pressure moments, like car rides, to start conversations.
They push back on every rule.	Involve them in setting boundaries and explain the reasoning behind rules. This gives them a sense of control and responsibility.
They seem overwhelmed by schoolwork and responsibilities.	Help them prioritise tasks by breaking them into manageable steps. Teach them time management skills, like using a planner or to-do list.
They're constantly comparing themselves to their peers.	Emphasise their unique strengths and accomplishments. Encourage them to focus on personal growth rather than competition.
They make impulsive or risky decisions.	Use mistakes as learning opportunities. Talk about consequences without judgment: "What do you think you could do differently next time?"
They struggle with self-esteem.	Validate their feelings and remind them of their value beyond achievements. Help them identify activities that build confidence and joy.
They resist family activities.	Let them help plan family time so they feel invested. Keep activities flexible and

	fun, like a movie night or cooking a meal together.

 Pro Tip for Troubleshooting

Teens are navigating identity, independence, and emotions. Your role shifts from manager to mentor—being present, listening without judgment, and guiding them toward confident adulthood is your ultimate cheat code.

Final Boss Battle:
Surviving Parenthood and Keeping Your Sanity Intact

Welcome to the Final Boss Battle

Player 1, you've made it to the endgame! After navigating countless levels, battling tantrums, eye rolls, and endless snack negotiations, you've reached the **Final Boss Battle: Surviving Parenthood and Keeping Your Sanity Intact**. This stage isn't about your child—it's about **you**.

Your mission: **Reflect on the journey, celebrate your wins, and keep growing alongside your child. Parenting doesn't end—it evolves.**

 Pro tip: Teenagers don't need you to fix everything—they need you to listen, respect their growing autonomy, and remind them you're always in their corner.

The Final Boss Battle: The Guilt Gremlin

The Guilt Gremlin is a tricky opponent. It sneaks in when you're reflecting on your parenting journey, whispering doubts like, "Did I do enough?" or "What if I messed them up?" It feeds on your self-doubt, threatening to overshadow your successes.

How to Defeat the Guilt Gremlin:

1. **Flip the Script:** When the Gremlin says, "You failed," respond with, "I learned." Mistakes are inevitable in parenting; what matters is how you grow from them.

2. **Celebrate the Wins:** Think about the moments you showed up, no matter how small—those are victories.

3. **Practice Self-Compassion:** Treat yourself with the kindness you'd show your child.

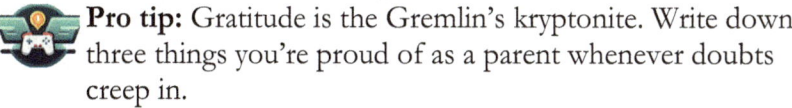 **Pro tip:** Gratitude is the Gremlin's kryptonite. Write down three things you're proud of as a parent whenever doubts creep in.

Gameplay Hazards

- **The Comparison Monster:**
  It whispers that other parents are doing better than you.
    - **How to Beat It:** Focus on your unique journey and remind yourself that no family is the same. Your love and effort matter most.

- **The "What-If" Wizard:**
  This sneaky trickster conjures regrets about the past and fears about the future.
    - **How to Beat It:** Stay grounded in the present. Parenting happens in the here and now.

- **The Empty Fuel Bar:**
  You've given so much to your child that you've forgotten to recharge yourself.
    - **How to Beat It:** Prioritize self-care—it's not selfish, it's essential. Take time for hobbies, friends, or even just quiet moments alone.

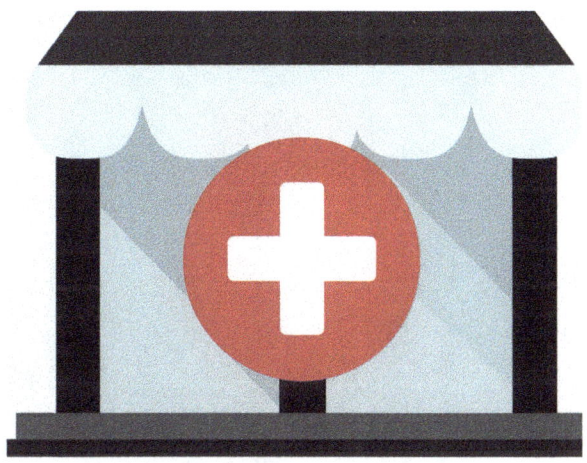

Cheat Codes

1. **The Reflection Buff:**
   Look back at the early levels and see how far you've come. Recognize the growth in your child—and in yourself.

2. **The Connection Treasure:**
   Even as your child grows, prioritise one-on-one time to maintain your bond. These moments keep the connection strong.

3. **The "Good Enough" Hack:**
   Let go of perfectionism. Your child doesn't need a perfect parent—they need a present one.

Save Point: The Bigger Picture

Parenting is a series of endless quests, each filled with challenges, triumphs, and plenty of retries. But it's also filled with **save points**—those moments of pure joy, laughter, and connection that remind you why it's all worth it. A heartfelt "thank you," an unexpected hug, or a shared laugh during the chaos can recharge your parenting energy bar and give you the strength to keep going. These moments may seem small, but they're the treasures that make the journey meaningful. They remind you that, even amid the messiness and uncertainty, you're creating something beautiful—a relationship built on love, trust, and connection. So, when the game feels hard, look for those save points. They're the rewards that make this adventure unforgettable.

 Pro tip: Keep finding and savouring these moments. They're the real treasure of the game.

 # Troubleshooting Guide

Issue	Fix
I feel like I didn't do enough.	Remind yourself that parenting isn't about being perfect; it's about showing up. Reflect on moments you did your best—and celebrate them.
I miss the early stages.	Nostalgia is natural. Use those feelings to celebrate how far your child has come and find joy in their current stage.
Parenting feels like it's never-ending.	Shift your mindset: It's not about finishing—it's about enjoying the ride. Focus on the connection, not the completion.
I feel disconnected from my child now that they're older.	Find shared interests or create new traditions. Even small rituals, like a weekly coffee date or family movie night, can reignite connection.
I don't know what my role is now.	Your role has evolved into mentor and supporter. Offer guidance when asked, and respect their growing independence.

 Pro Tip for Troubleshooting

Parenting is a marathon, not a sprint. Your mistakes don't define you—your willingness to learn and keep showing up does. Celebrate the small wins and remember: good enough is more than enough.

Epilogue: The Journey Continues

Parenting doesn't have a true "Game Over." Instead, it's a lifelong journey of evolving roles, growing connections, and shared experiences. Each level brought its own challenges and rewards, and while the quests change, the bond you've built with your child remains constant.

You've navigated The Parenting Game with resilience, love, and humour. And remember: every parent learns as they go. You're leveling up every day, and that's something to be proud of.

Achievement Unlocked: Parenthood Complete (For Now).

Afterword: The Parenting Game—Why Connection Matters

Parenting is the ultimate open-world game: there are no maps, no clear instructions, and certainly no pause button. Just when you think you've figured out one level, the game shifts, introducing new challenges, mini-bosses, and the occasional (or frequent) tantrum. And yet, it's the most immersive, life-changing adventure you'll ever undertake.

In *The Parenting Game*, we wanted to capture the essence of this journey—not as a manual that promises perfection (because that's not real) but as a guide to help you navigate the ups, downs, and sideways twists with humour, heart, and a little more clarity. Why gaming as a theme? Because parenting is a lot like a video game: it's messy, unpredictable, and at times frustrating, but it's also joyful, rewarding, and full of "Save Point" moments that make it all worthwhile.

Why We Wrote This Book
Between the two of us, we've logged over 40 years in education and 16 years in the trenches of parenting. We've taught thousands of children, worked with their families, and parented our own kids through meltdowns, eye-rolls, and awkward school photos. What we've learned through these experiences is simple but profound: **connection is the foundation of everything.**

Whether you're navigating Level 1 with a newborn or bracing yourself for the Final Boss Battle with a teenager, the same principle holds true: your child's sense of security, resilience, and authenticity comes from knowing you're there for them. The way you show up—imperfectly but consistently—has a profound impact not just on their childhood but on who they'll become as adults.

But we also know this is easier said than done. Parenting is hard, messy, and often feels like stumbling through a dark cave with no torch. That's why we structured this book the way we did: to provide both practical tools and a light-hearted framework to help you navigate the adventure without losing your sanity (or your sense of humour).

The Two Core Themes: Attachment and Authenticity.

At its heart, *The Parenting Game* is built around two interconnected themes: **attachment** and **authenticity.** These aren't just buzzwords; they're the guiding stars of effective, connected parenting.

1. **Attachment:**
    - In the early levels of parenting, attachment is everything. When your baby cries, they're asking one fundamental question: "Is someone here for me?" Your response teaches them that the world is safe and that they can trust others.
    - This isn't about being perfect. Attachment is built through small, everyday moments: locking eyes during a feeding, rocking them to sleep, or responding to their cries with a calming touch. These acts, repeated consistently (not flawlessly), wire your child's brain for security and resilience.

2. **Authenticity:**
    - As your child grows, the balance begins to shift. The toddler who once clung to your leg now insists on pouring their own cereal. The school-age child starts defining themselves outside the family. The teenager challenges your rules, beliefs, and patience.
    - These are good things. Your child's authenticity—their ability to know and express who they truly are—depends on your willingness to let go, step back, and support their independence.

The trick is balancing these themes. Attachment and authenticity aren't opposites; they're complementary. A securely attached child feels safe enough to explore the world and be themselves, knowing that no matter what, you'll always be their anchor.

Why Humour Matters.

Let's be real: parenting can be absurd. One minute you're trying to have a deep conversation with your teenager about respect, and the next, you're stepping on a rogue LEGO in your bare feet. One moment your toddler is giggling uncontrollably, and the next, they're on the floor screaming because their banana broke in half. Humour isn't just a coping mechanism—it's a parenting superpower. It diffuses tension, strengthens connection, and reminds us not to take ourselves too seriously. That's why this book doesn't shy away from the ridiculousness of parenting. We believe that laughing at the chaos doesn't diminish its importance—it makes it more bearable.

The Importance of Play.

We've seen it time and time again in classrooms, at home, and in our own lives: **play is where connection happens.** That's why we included side quests in every level. These aren't just cute activities to kill time—they're intentional opportunities to bond, spark joy, and create memories.

- In Level 1, tummy time isn't just about strengthening muscles; it's about cheering on your baby as they learn to lift their head, showing them that you're their biggest fan.
- In Level 4, a DIY game night isn't just a way to avoid screen time; it's a chance to collaborate, laugh, and remind your child that family time is fun.
- Play evolves as your child grows, but its purpose remains the same: to build connection and trust in ways words alone can't.

Mistakes Are Part of the Game.

If there's one thing we want you to take away from this book, it's this: **you don't have to get it right every time.** Parenting isn't about perfection—it's about showing up, learning as you go, and repairing when you miss the mark.

The truth is, you will make mistakes. You'll lose your patience, say the wrong thing, or feel like you're failing. And that's okay. Mistakes are inevitable, but repair is powerful. Apologising, reconnecting, and trying again teaches your child that relationships are resilient—and so are you.

Why the Gaming Metaphor?

We didn't choose the gaming metaphor just because it's fun (though it is). We chose it because it reflects the reality of parenting:

- **Levels:** Each stage of your child's development brings new challenges and opportunities.
- **Big Bosses and Mini-Bosses:** From sleep deprivation to teenage rebellion, the obstacles are real, but they're also surmountable.
- **Cheat Codes:** Every parent needs a few life hacks to make the game easier.
- **Save Points:** These are the moments of connection, laughter, and pride that keep you going when the game gets tough.

Parenting isn't linear, and it doesn't have a "win state." It's a lifelong adventure, full of respawns, retries, and rewards. The gaming framework is our way of making this journey feel less daunting and more like what it is: an epic quest.

The Big Picture.

At its core, parenting is about building a relationship. It's not about raising a "perfect" child or being a "perfect" parent—it's about creating a bond that can weather tantrums, mistakes, and hard conversations. It's about showing your child, over and over, that they are loved, valued, and seen.

As educators and parents, we've witnessed the transformative power of connection. We've seen the child who struggles with schoolwork but thrives under a teacher who believes in them.

We've seen the teenager who tests every boundary but softens when their parent says, "I'm here if you need me." And we've felt it in our own lives—in the messy, magical, imperfect moments that make parenting so challenging and so worth it.

The New 3Rs: Role-Modelling, Resilience, and *Not* Rescuing.

Parenting today feels like navigating a tightrope. On one side is the instinct to protect—to smooth every bump, soothe every hurt, and solve every problem. On the other side is the need to foster independence—to equip our children to walk their own paths, face their own challenges, and build resilience. The balance is delicate, but crucial. In this chapter, we'll explore the new 3Rs of parenting: Role-Modelling, Resilience, and Not Rescuing. Together, these principles can help us raise capable, compassionate, and confident children in a world that often feels overwhelming.

Role-Modelling: They Learn What We Live

Our children are always watching. More than our words, it's our actions that shape their understanding of how to move through the world. If we tell them to be present, but are constantly checking our phones, the lesson they learn is that distraction is acceptable. If we encourage them to be curious but respond to their endless questions with sighs of frustration, they learn that curiosity is a burden.

Role-modelling means living the behaviours we want to instil. It's about demonstrating patience when the queue at the supermarket crawls, empathy when a neighbour is struggling, and curiosity when we stop to marvel at a starry night sky. It also means modelling vulnerability—sharing stories of our own childhood struggles, the mistakes we made, and how we learned from them.

For instance, if your child is anxious about presenting at school, resist the urge to dismiss their fear with "You'll be fine." Instead, share your own experience: "I remember feeling nervous before work presentations. I even felt my heart race. Here's what helped me: I took a deep breath, focused on one friendly face, and reminded myself I'd prepared well." In that moment, you've role-modelled vulnerability, emotional regulation, and problem-solving.

Psychologist Albert Bandura's social learning theory highlights that children learn behaviours through observation, imitation, and modelling. When they see us manage stress calmly, engage with curiosity, and practice kindness, they are more likely to replicate those behaviours.

Another practical example: if you want your child to develop healthy digital habits, start by examining your own. Are you scrolling through your phone during conversations? Try setting up family-wide screen-free times, like during dinner or before bed. When children witness parents setting boundaries with technology, they're more likely to follow suit.

Resilience: Built Through Safe, Supported Struggles

Resilience isn't something a child magically develops in isolation. It grows when children face challenges with the scaffolding of a safe, supportive adult beside them. Too often, resilience is misunderstood as toughness or independence. In reality, resilience is the ability to bounce back because a child knows they have a secure foundation to fall back on.

When a toddler falls while learning to walk, we instinctively smile and say, "Oops! Up you get!" We don't berate them for falling or rush to carry them everywhere. The same principle applies as they grow older. When they forget their lunchbox, resist the urge to drop it off at school. Instead, use it as an opportunity to brainstorm strategies together: "What could help you remember tomorrow? Maybe we could put a sticky note on the front door or set an alarm."

The discomfort of natural consequences, paired with compassionate guidance, becomes the training ground for resilience. They learn I can handle challenges. I can solve problems. I am supported, but capable.

Dr. Gabor Maté emphasizes the importance of co-regulation: children borrow our calm when they are distressed. A study published in Developmental Psychology found that children who had parents who coached them through emotional challenges were better able to manage stress later in life. This highlights that resilience is not a solo Endeavor—it is co-created through relationship.

Practical examples can make this abstract concept clearer. Imagine a child struggling with a difficult homework assignment. The instinct might be to sit down and help solve each problem. A more resilience-building approach is to sit nearby and say, "This looks challenging. What's your plan to tackle it? Want to brainstorm some strategies together?" The child learns problem-solving without feeling abandoned.

Not Rescuing: Guiding, Not Fixing

The desire to rescue our children from discomfort is deeply human. No parent wants to see their child hurt, frustrated, or anxious. Yet, when we habitually step in to fix things, we inadvertently send the message: "You can't handle this." Over time, children either become dependent on us to solve their problems or internalize a belief that the world is too overwhelming for them.

Not rescuing doesn't mean abandoning. It means sitting beside them in their discomfort, offering empathy, and guiding them toward solutions. Picture a child struggling with a friendship issue. The rescuing response might be to call the other child's parent or suggest they find new friends. The non-rescuing response is to sit alongside, listen, and ask: "What do you think might help here? Want to brainstorm some ideas together?"

In adolescence, this principle becomes even more critical. If your teenager wants a part-time job, don't phone businesses on their behalf. Instead, help them create a resume, role-play interview scenarios, and talk through potential challenges. When they land the job, the pride they feel will be rooted in their effort—not in your intervention.

We can't understate the importance of connection in overcoming life's difficulties. By supporting children to face challenges side-by-side, rather than removing obstacles for them, we foster both their resilience and their trust in us as dependable guides.

The Power of Affirmation and Avoiding Shame

Throughout this process, our language matters. Children learn best in an environment where mistakes are seen as part of growth, not as failures to be ashamed of. Avoiding shame doesn't mean avoiding accountability. It means framing mistakes as learning opportunities.

Instead of, "Why can't you remember your bag?" try, "Packing your bag can be tricky—what might help you remember tomorrow?"

Affirm their feelings, even when those feelings are hard to witness. If they say, "I hate school," resist the urge to correct or dismiss. Instead, respond with curiosity: "That sounds tough. What's been hard about it lately?" This approach builds trust, teaches emotional intelligence, and communicates that all emotions are normal and manageable.

Andrew Lines, who developed the Rites of Passage Framework, emphasizes the importance of helping children navigate life's challenges while affirming their inherent worth. When parents respond to distress with empathy rather than dismissal, children learn that all emotions are valid and manageable.

Our Own Baggage: Parenting from Self-Awareness

Finally, parenting with the new 3Rs requires self-awareness. Our own childhood experiences shape how we respond to our children's struggles. If we were raised to "just get on with it," we might dismiss our child's emotions. If we were excessively protected, we might overcorrect by pushing independence too soon.

Take time to reflect: How did your parents handle discomfort? What messages did you internalize about mistakes, emotions, and challenges? When we parent from a place of awareness rather than reaction, we can consciously choose responses that align with our long-term goals for our children.

Mel Robbins often speaks about the power of modelling self-awareness. If we notice ourselves reacting harshly, we can pause, name the feeling, and later share with our child: "I was really stressed earlier and snapped. I'm sorry about that. I'm working on taking deep breaths when I feel overwhelmed." In doing so, we model both accountability and emotional regulation.

Conclusion: Walking Beside, Not Carrying

The new 3Rs—Role-Modelling, Resilience, and Not Rescuing—are not about perfection. We will all have moments of impatience, worry, or intervention. The goal is to shift our default from fixing to guiding, from telling to showing, from rescuing to reassuring.

When we walk beside our children instead of carrying them, we give them the greatest gift: the belief that they can navigate life's challenges with courage, creativity, and confidence—because they've seen it modelled, practiced it with support, and experienced the pride of overcoming difficulties on their own.

For those with more time! (Informative and inspirational reads)

Bandura, A. (1977). Social Learning Theory. Prentice Hall.

Maté, G. (2008). In the Realm of Hungry Ghosts: Close Encounters with Addiction. Knopf Canada.

Hari, J. (2018). Lost Connections: Uncovering the Real Causes of Depression – and the Unexpected Solutions. Bloomsbury Publishing.

Lines, A. The Rites of Passage Framework (various publications).

Robbins, M. (2017). The 5 Second Rule: Transform your Life, Work, and Confidence with Everyday Courage. Savio Republic.

A Final Word.

If you've made it this far in the book, thank you. Thank you for showing up for your child, for seeking tools to navigate this adventure, and for trusting us to be part of your parenting journey. Whether you're just starting out or facing the Final Boss, remember this: You're doing better than you think.
Parenting is the hardest game you'll ever play, but it's also the most rewarding. And while there's no pause button, there are plenty of Save Points. Keep finding them. Keep savouring them. And most of all, keep playing.

Achievement Unlocked: You're an incredible parent.

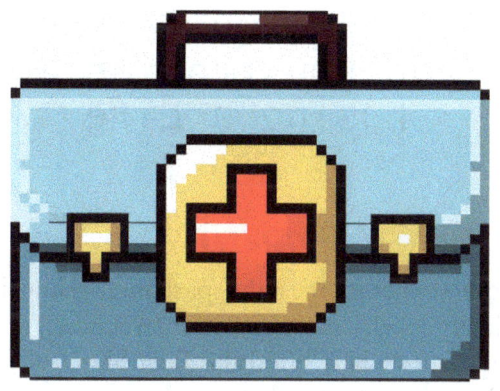

Tear out in case of emergency!

HELP...

...This is not what I signed up for!

Parenting Rage Quit: Navigating Anger and Frustration Without Losing a Life

Let's be honest: sometimes the parenting game is set to the hardest difficulty level—no map, no instructions, and a constant barrage of side quests like "Find the Lost Shoe" and "Why is the Milk in the Pantry?" Anger and frustration are part of the package. If you've picked up this book mid-rage, welcome. You're exactly where you need to be.

Step 1: Press Pause

First, stop. Breathe. You don't have to solve this right now. Anger makes us reactive, not reflective. It's like when your kid does something ridiculous, and you're standing there thinking, 'Why...why are you like this?' And then you remember: oh yeah, they share my DNA.

Quick Pause Tricks:

The 5-5-5 Breath: Inhale for 5 seconds, hold for 5, exhale for 5. Repeat until your inner voice says, "Aye, calm doon."

The Angry Cup of Tea: Announce, "I'm making a cup of tea to save us both." Bonus: your child learns that emotions can be managed, not unleashed.

The Exit Stage Left: If safe, step outside for a moment. There's no problem so big that you can't walk away from it for a minute...except maybe stepping on Lego.

Step 2: Decode the Rage Monster

Anger is often a surface emotion, with worry, exhaustion, or unmet expectations lurking underneath. Anger protects our boundaries. But when we parent from it, we lose connection.

Ask Yourself:

What boundary was crossed? (Respect, safety, sanity?)

What do I actually need here? (Quiet, cooperation, fewer existential questions at bedtime?)

What's going on with my child? (Are they tired, overwhelmed, or testing limits?)

And here's a gem: sometimes we're angry because kids are just...kids. Like when your three-year-old insists on putting shoes on the dog because "he wants to go to the park." He doesn't. He wants his dignity back.

Step 3: Deploy the Humour Hack

Humour diffuses tension like nothing else. Laughter doesn't just lighten the mood—it gives you a mental reset and reminds everyone that you're a team, not opponents.

Tactical Humour Moves:

The Silly Reset: Do an over-the-top fake meltdown: "Oh no! The dishwasher's not unloaded! The world will end!" Guaranteed eye-rolls but also laughter.

The Accent Challenge: Deliver your next instruction in a ridiculous accent. Try "Brush your teeth" with a pirate growl.

The Shared Joke: "I need a break before I turn into Grumpy McParentface."

Someone has always had it worse!
My friend once spent an entire evening looking for her son's school library book called The Sneaky Squirrel. She tore the house apart. Next morning, her son casually announced, "Oh yeah, I buried it in the garden so the squirrel could find its family."

Laughter doesn't erase the frustration, but it shrinks it down to a manageable size.

Step 4: Repair, Don't Ruminate

We all lose it sometimes. What matters is what comes next.

The Parenting Repair Script:

"I was really frustrated earlier and I yelled. I'm sorry for that. Let's figure out how to solve this together."

"Everyone gets angry—it's a normal feeling. The trick is learning what to do with it. Want to brainstorm our own Anger Playbook?"

"I love you, even when I'm mad. Always."

Someone has always had it worse!
A dad I know tried to apologise for yelling at his son. The kid said, "It's okay, Dad. I've heard worse on YouTube." Cue a family meeting on internet safety.

Step 5: Build an Anger Game Plan

Think of this as a cheat code for next time.

Anger Playbook Checklist:

Trigger ID: What situations push your buttons? (Homework refusal, bedtime debates, "Can I have a snack?" three seconds after dinner.)

Pause Plan: What will you do when anger flares? (Breath, tea, a quick "walk-off" like a footballer protesting a red card.)

Communicate Calm: How will you explain your feelings to your child without blame? ("I need a minute to cool down because I want to talk calmly with you.")

Practice Together: Help your child create their own anger plan. Show them that emotional self-regulation is a skill, not magic.

Someone has always had it worse!
A mum told me her teenager was always forgetting lunch. One day she said, "Fine, you'll figure it out." The kid did—by ordering a triple cheeseburger, fries, and a smoothie delivered to school. Lesson learned: resilience isn't always nutritious.

Parenting Is a Contact Sport (Emotionally, at Least)

Anger isn't failure. It's a sign that you care. You're not alone—every parent has their "I'm gonna lose it" moments. There's no such thing as bad weather, just bad clothes. In parenting terms: there's no such thing as a bad parent, just a parent learning new emotional gear.

So go on—breathe, laugh, and know that turning this page instead of turning into the Hulk? That's already a parenting win.

Resources:

Survival Pack

Strategies for Every Schedule

This section offers **10-minute**, **30-minute**, and **1-hour** self-care ideas for busy parents. Think of them as "power-ups" to keep you feeling balanced and recharged during the parenting game.

10-Minute Power-Ups

- ☐ **The Breathing Boost:** Close your eyes, inhale deeply for 4 seconds, hold for 4, exhale for 4, and repeat for 5 cycles.
- ☐ **Coffee or Tea Time-Out:** Sip your favourite drink—slowly, without multitasking.
- ☐ **Gratitude Snapshot:** Write down 3 things you're grateful for today, even if they're small wins.
- ☐ **Micro-Meditation:** Use a meditation app or a calming playlist for a quick mental reset.
- ☐ **Sunshine Sprint:** Step outside for fresh air and a quick walk around the block.
- ☐ **Stretch to Reset:** Do 5 stretches focusing on your back, shoulders, and neck.
- ☐ **Laugh Break:** Watch a short, funny video or read a few pages from a humorous book.
- ☐ **Mini-Journal:** Write down one thought or feeling to process and release it.
- ☐ **Dance Break:** Put on an energising song and move like nobody's watching.
- ☐ **Skin Reset:** Apply a face mask or simply splash cold water on your face for an instant refresh.

30-Minute Power-Ups

- ☐ **Yoga Flow:** Follow a 20–30 minute yoga video focusing on relaxation or energy.
- ☐ **Unplug and Read:** Pick up a book or magazine you love—bonus points if it's unrelated to parenting!
- ☐ **Nature Recharge:** Take a leisurely walk in a park or sit in your backyard with a cup of tea.
- ☐ **Call a Friend:** Connect with someone who makes you feel supported or inspired.
- ☐ **Creative Escape:** Draw, write, bake, or engage in a hobby that brings you joy.
- ☐ **Bubble Bath Bliss:** Light a candle, put on calming music, and soak away the stress.
- ☐ **Meal Prep Zen:** Prepare a simple, nourishing meal or snack just for yourself.
- ☐ **Declutter One Space:** Tidy a small area, like a drawer or your desk, for a mental refresh.
- ☐ **Guided Meditation or Mindfulness Session:** Use an app or YouTube to dive deeper into relaxation.
- ☐ **Exercise Burst:** Do a home workout or brisk walk to get your heart pumping.

1-Hour Power-ups

- ☐ **Spa at Home:** Take a long bath, exfoliate, moisturise, and indulge in a mini spa treatment.
- ☐ **Go Solo:** Visit a café or bookstore alone for uninterrupted "me" time.
- ☐ **Mindful Meal:** Cook and savour a meal at your own pace, with zero interruptions.
- ☐ **Movie Escape:** Watch a feel-good movie or TV episode—guilt-free!
- ☐ **Date with a Hobby:** Paint, knit, garden, play music, or dive into something that's purely yours.
- ☐ **Power Nap:** Give yourself permission to nap and recharge fully.
- ☐ **Nature Immersion:** Go for a hike or a longer stroll in a calming natural setting.
- ☐ **Podcast and Chill:** Listen to an inspiring or entertaining podcast while relaxing.
- ☐ **Deep Declutter:** Organize a space that's been bothering you—like your closet or pantry.
- ☐ **Workout or Class:** Attend a fitness class, swim, or dedicate an hour to your favourite exercise.

QR Code References

Listen   *Watch*

Level 1

Podcast:
"The Birth Hour"
This podcast shares birth stories and experiences, offering support and insights for new parents navigating the early months.
[Thriving Mum](#)

YouTube Video:
"Dr Karp 5 S"
Swaddle, Side position, Shush, Swing, Suck (a pacifier or feed).
[Dr Karp 5 s's](#)

"The Single Most Important Parenting Strategy"
Clinical psychologist Dr. Becky Kennedy discusses effective parenting strategies.
[YouTube](#)

Level 2

Podcast:
"Respectful Parenting: Janet Lansbury Unruffled"
Janet Lansbury addresses common toddler behaviours and offers respectful parenting advice.
[Mighty Kids Academy](#)

YouTube Video:
"Master Positive Parenting: 10 Expert Tips"
This video provides practical tips for positive parenting during the toddler years.
[YouTube](#)

Level 3

Podcast:
"But Why: A Podcast for Curious Kids"
This podcast answers questions from curious kids, making it perfect for preschoolers and their parents.
Parents

YouTube Video:
"Your Child's Behaviour | 5 to 6 Years | Good Parenting Videos"
This video offers insights into managing behaviours typical of preschool-aged children.
YouTube

Level 4

Podcast:
"Mom and Dad Are Fighting"
Hosted by Slate, this podcast provides advice for parenting school-aged children.
Parents

YouTube Video:
"Listening to the Heart of Your Kids"
This video emphasises the importance of listening to your children during the school years.
YouTube

Level 5

Podcast:
"Good Inside with Dr. Becky"
Clinical psychologist Dr. Becky Kennedy offers parenting advice relevant to the tween years.
Parents

YouTube Video:
"5 Expert Tips No Parent Should Miss | Positive Parenting"
This video compiles expert advice beneficial for parents of tweens.
YouTube

Level 6

Podcast:
"Talking to Teens: Expert Tips for Parenting Teenagers"
This podcast offers insights and advice for parents navigating the teenage years.
Parents

YouTube Video:
"The Single Most Important Parenting Strategy"
Dr. Becky Kennedy discusses strategies that are also applicable to parenting teenagers.
YouTube

Notes & Scribbles

This space is yours. Use it to jot down insights, ideas, or just vent about the madness of parenting. Write down the brilliant parenting hack you invented at 2 a.m. Or the hilarious moment when your child announced, "Mum, I think the dog needs therapy."

Parenting isn't about perfection; it's about presence. And sometimes presence requires a bit of scribbling space.

(Feel free to doodle too. Stick-figure family portraits encouraged.)

Kids Say the Funniest Things: A Space to Capture the Moments We Swear We'll Remember

Children have a magical ability to say the most hilarious, profound, and downright bizarre things—usually when we least expect it. We always promise ourselves we'll remember, but life moves on, and those little gems get lost.

Here's your spot. Scribble down the quirky quotes, the unexpected wisdom, and the laugh-out-loud moments. Whether it's the time they confidently declared, "I don't need a bedtime—I'm basically nocturnal now" or asked, "Why don't penguins wear socks?", these are the stories you'll want to revisit when they're taller, older, and definitely less interested in bedtime cuddles.

(Bonus tip: Read these back to your kids when they're teenagers. Embarrassment guaranteed.)

Parenting Wins Log

Space to record moments when they nailed it.

www.ingramcontent.com/pod-product-compliance
Lightning Source LLC
Chambersburg PA
CBHW070549090426
42735CB00013B/3121